This Journal

Belongs To:

ASMA UL HUSNA
JOURNAL

BY MUSLIM JOURNALS

*This journal was crafted from the heart
with artful detail from us to you.
Your satisfaction is very important, so for any
issues with your journal please contact:
hello@muslimjournals.com*

"Indeed, Allah has Ninety-Nine Names - one hundred minus one - whoever encompasses them will enter Paradise."

- BUKHARI (HADITH)

Allah's Beautiful Names

>>>———————————————————→

DATE:

The Beautiful Name Of Allah:

Meaning Of Allah's Name:

Allah's Name In The Quran:

Explanation Of Allah's Name:

My Reflection Of Allah's Name:

"Call upon Allah or call upon the Most Merciful. Whichever (Name) you call - to Him belong the best names." - The Quran 17:110

Allah's Beautiful Names

⇛⟶

DATE:

The Beautiful Name Of Allah:

Meaning Of Allah's Name:

Allah's Name In The Quran:

Explanation Of Allah's Name:

My Reflection Of Allah's Name:

"Call upon Allah or call upon the Most Merciful. Whichever (Name) you call - to Him belong the best names." - The Quran 17:110

Allah's Beautiful Names

>>>———————————————————→

DATE:

The Beautiful Name Of Allah:

Meaning Of Allah's Name:

Allah's Name In The Quran:

Explanation Of Allah's Name:

My Reflection Of Allah's Name:

"Call upon Allah or call upon the Most Merciful. Whichever (Name) you call - to Him belong the best names." - The Quran 17:110

Allah's Beautiful Names

>>>———————————————→

DATE:

The Beautiful Name Of Allah:

Meaning Of Allah's Name:

Allah's Name In The Quran:

Explanation Of Allah's Name:

My Reflection Of Allah's Name:

"Call upon Allah or call upon the Most Merciful. Whichever (Name) you call - to Him belong the best names." - The Quran 17:110

Allah's Beautiful Names

$\ggg\!\longrightarrow$

DATE:

The Beautiful Name Of Allah:

Meaning Of Allah's Name:

Allah's Name In The Quran:

Explanation Of Allah's Name:

My Reflection Of Allah's Name:

"Call upon Allah or call upon the Most Merciful. Whichever (Name) you call - to Him belong the best names." - The Quran 17:110

Allah's Beautiful Names

>>>———————————————————→

DATE:

The Beautiful Name Of Allah:

Meaning Of Allah's Name:

Allah's Name In The Quran:

Explanation Of Allah's Name:

My Reflection Of Allah's Name:

"Call upon Allah or call upon the Most Merciful. Whichever (Name) you call - to Him belong the best names." - The Quran 17:110

Allah's Beautiful Names

>>>———————————————→

DATE:

The Beautiful Name Of Allah:

Meaning Of Allah's Name:

Allah's Name In The Quran:

Explanation Of Allah's Name:

My Reflection Of Allah's Name:

"Call upon Allah or call upon the Most Merciful. Whichever (Name) you call - to Him belong the best names." - The Quran 17:110

Allah's Beautiful Names

>>> ———————————————————→

DATE:

The Beautiful Name Of Allah:

Meaning Of Allah's Name:

Allah's Name In The Quran:

Explanation Of Allah's Name:

My Reflection Of Allah's Name:

"Call upon Allah or call upon the Most Merciful. Whichever (Name) you call - to Him belong the best names." - The Quran 17:110

Allah's Beautiful Names

>>>————————————————————→

DATE:

The Beautiful Name Of Allah:

Meaning Of Allah's Name:

Allah's Name In The Quran:

Explanation Of Allah's Name:

My Reflection Of Allah's Name:

"Call upon Allah or call upon the Most Merciful. Whichever (Name) you call - to Him belong the best names." - The Quran 17:110

Allah's Beautiful Names

>>> ⟶

DATE:

The Beautiful Name Of Allah:

Meaning Of Allah's Name:

Allah's Name In The Quran:

Explanation Of Allah's Name:

My Reflection Of Allah's Name:

"Call upon Allah or call upon the Most Merciful. Whichever (Name) you call - to Him belong the best names." - The Quran 17:110

Allah's Beautiful Names

DATE:

The Beautiful Name Of Allah:

Meaning Of Allah's Name:

Allah's Name In The Quran:

Explanation Of Allah's Name:

My Reflection Of Allah's Name:

"Call upon Allah or call upon the Most Merciful. Whichever (Name) you call - to Him belong the best names." - The Quran 17:110

Allah's Beautiful Names

>>>———————————————————→

DATE:

The Beautiful Name Of Allah:

Meaning Of Allah's Name:

Allah's Name In The Quran:

Explanation Of Allah's Name:

My Reflection Of Allah's Name:

"Call upon Allah or call upon the Most Merciful. Whichever (Name) you call - to Him belong the best names." - The Quran 17:110

Allah's Beautiful Names

⫸⫸⫸━━━━━━━━━━━━━━━━━━━━━━━➤

DATE:

The Beautiful Name Of Allah:

Meaning Of Allah's Name:

Allah's Name In The Quran:

Explanation Of Allah's Name:

My Reflection Of Allah's Name:

"Call upon Allah or call upon the Most Merciful. Whichever (Name) you call - to Him belong the best names." - The Quran 17:110

Allah's Beautiful Names

>>>———————————————→

DATE:

The Beautiful Name Of Allah:

Meaning Of Allah's Name:

Allah's Name In The Quran:

Explanation Of Allah's Name:

My Reflection Of Allah's Name:

"Call upon Allah or call upon the Most Merciful. Whichever (Name) you call - to Him belong the best names." - The Quran 17:110

Allah's Beautiful Names

>>>————————————————→

DATE:

The Beautiful Name Of Allah:

Meaning Of Allah's Name:

Allah's Name In The Quran:

Explanation Of Allah's Name:

My Reflection Of Allah's Name:

"Call upon Allah or call upon the Most Merciful. Whichever (Name) you call - to Him belong the best names." - The Quran 17:110

Allah's Beautiful Names

>>> →

DATE:

The Beautiful Name Of Allah:

Meaning Of Allah's Name:

Allah's Name In The Quran:

Explanation Of Allah's Name:

My Reflection Of Allah's Name:

"Call upon Allah or call upon the Most Merciful. Whichever (Name) you call - to Him belong the best names." - The Quran 17:110

Allah's Beautiful Names

>>>————————————————→

DATE:

The Beautiful Name Of Allah:

Meaning Of Allah's Name:

Allah's Name In The Quran:

Explanation Of Allah's Name:

My Reflection Of Allah's Name:

"Call upon Allah or call upon the Most Merciful. Whichever (Name) you call - to Him belong the best names." - The Quran 17:110

Allah's Beautiful Names

>>>————————————————————→

DATE:

The Beautiful Name Of Allah:

Meaning Of Allah's Name:

Allah's Name In The Quran:

My Reflection Of Allah's Name:

"Call upon Allah or call upon the Most Merciful. Whichever (Name) you call - to Him belong the best names." - The Quran 17:110

Allah's Beautiful Names

>>>————————————————————→

DATE:

The Beautiful Name Of Allah:

Meaning Of Allah's Name:

Allah's Name In The Quran:

Explanation Of Allah's Name:

My Reflection Of Allah's Name:

"Call upon Allah or call upon the Most Merciful. Whichever (Name) you call - to Him belong the best names." - The Quran 17:110

Allah's Beautiful Names

DATE:

The Beautiful Name Of Allah:

Meaning Of Allah's Name:

Allah's Name In The Quran:

Explanation Of Allah's Name:

My Reflection Of Allah's Name:

"Call upon Allah or call upon the Most Merciful. Whichever (Name) you call - to Him belong the best names." - The Quran 17:110

Allah's Beautiful Names

>>>———————————————————→

DATE:

The Beautiful Name Of Allah:

Meaning Of Allah's Name:

Allah's Name In The Quran:

Explanation Of Allah's Name:

My Reflection Of Allah's Name:

"Call upon Allah or call upon the Most Merciful. Whichever (Name) you call - to Him belong the best names." - The Quran 17:110

Allah's Beautiful Names

>>> ⟶

DATE:

The Beautiful Name Of Allah:

Meaning Of Allah's Name:

Allah's Name In The Quran:

Explanation Of Allah's Name:

My Reflection Of Allah's Name:

"Call upon Allah or call upon the Most Merciful. Whichever (Name) you call - to Him belong the best names." - The Quran 17:110

Allah's Beautiful Names

>>>⟶

DATE:

The Beautiful Name Of Allah:

Meaning Of Allah's Name:

Allah's Name In The Quran:

Explanation Of Allah's Name:

My Reflection Of Allah's Name:

"Call upon Allah or call upon the Most Merciful. Whichever (Name) you call - to Him belong the best names." - The Quran 17:110

Allah's Beautiful Names

>>> ———————————————→

DATE:

The Beautiful Name Of Allah:

Meaning Of Allah's Name:

Allah's Name In The Quran:

Explanation Of Allah's Name:

My Reflection Of Allah's Name:

"Call upon Allah or call upon the Most Merciful. Whichever (Name) you call - to Him belong the best names." - The Quran 17:110

Allah's Beautiful Names

>>>———————————————————→

DATE:

The Beautiful Name Of Allah:

Meaning Of Allah's Name:

Allah's Name In The Quran:

Explanation Of Allah's Name:

My Reflection Of Allah's Name:

"Call upon Allah or call upon the Most Merciful. Whichever (Name) you call - to Him belong the best names." - The Quran 17:110

Allah's Beautiful Names

>>>———————————————→

DATE:

The Beautiful Name Of Allah:

Meaning Of Allah's Name:

Allah's Name In The Quran:

Explanation Of Allah's Name:

My Reflection Of Allah's Name:

"Call upon Allah or call upon the Most Merciful. Whichever (Name) you call - to Him belong the best names." - The Quran 17:110

Allah's Beautiful Names

>>>————————————————————————→

DATE:

The Beautiful Name Of Allah:

Meaning Of Allah's Name:

Allah's Name In The Quran:

Explanation Of Allah's Name:

My Reflection Of Allah's Name:

"Call upon Allah or call upon the Most Merciful. Whichever (Name) you call - to Him belong the best names." - The Quran 17:110

Allah's Beautiful Names

>>>———————————————→

DATE:

The Beautiful Name Of Allah:

Meaning Of Allah's Name:

Allah's Name In The Quran:

Explanation Of Allah's Name:

My Reflection Of Allah's Name:

"Call upon Allah or call upon the Most Merciful. Whichever (Name) you call - to Him belong the best names." - The Quran 17:110

Allah's Beautiful Names

>>>———————————————————→

DATE:

The Beautiful Name Of Allah:

Meaning Of Allah's Name:

Allah's Name In The Quran:

Explanation Of Allah's Name:

My Reflection Of Allah's Name:

"Call upon Allah or call upon the Most Merciful. Whichever (Name) you call - to Him belong the best names." - The Quran 17:110

Allah's Beautiful Names

>>>───────────────────────────────→

DATE:

The Beautiful Name Of Allah:

Meaning Of Allah's Name:

Allah's Name In The Quran:

Explanation Of Allah's Name:

My Reflection Of Allah's Name:

"Call upon Allah or call upon the Most Merciful. Whichever (Name)
you call - to Him belong the best names." - The Quran 17:110

Allah's Beautiful Names

>>>———————————————→

DATE:

The Beautiful Name Of Allah:

Meaning Of Allah's Name:

Allah's Name In The Quran:

Explanation Of Allah's Name:

My Reflection Of Allah's Name:

"Call upon Allah or call upon the Most Merciful. Whichever (Name) you call - to Him belong the best names." - The Quran 17:110

Allah's Beautiful Names

>>>———————————————————>

DATE:

The Beautiful Name Of Allah:

Meaning Of Allah's Name:

Allah's Name In The Quran:

Explanation Of Allah's Name:

My Reflection Of Allah's Name:

"Call upon Allah or call upon the Most Merciful. Whichever (Name) you call - to Him belong the best names." - The Quran 17:110

Allah's Beautiful Names

>>>———————————————————→

DATE:

The Beautiful Name Of Allah:

Meaning Of Allah's Name:

Allah's Name In The Quran:

Explanation Of Allah's Name:

My Reflection Of Allah's Name:

"Call upon Allah or call upon the Most Merciful. Whichever (Name) you call - to Him belong the best names." - The Quran 17:110

Allah's Beautiful Names

$\ggg$ —————————————————→

DATE:

The Beautiful Name Of Allah:

Meaning Of Allah's Name:

Allah's Name In The Quran:

Explanation Of Allah's Name:

My Reflection Of Allah's Name:

"Call upon Allah or call upon the Most Merciful. Whichever (Name) you call - to Him belong the best names." - The Quran 17:110

Allah's Beautiful Names

>>>————————————————————→

DATE:

The Beautiful Name Of Allah:

Meaning Of Allah's Name:

Allah's Name In The Quran:

Explanation Of Allah's Name:

My Reflection Of Allah's Name:

"Call upon Allah or call upon the Most Merciful. Whichever (Name) you call - to Him belong the best names." - The Quran 17:110

Allah's Beautiful Names

>>>———————————————————→

DATE:

The Beautiful Name Of Allah:

Meaning Of Allah's Name:

Allah's Name In The Quran:

Explanation Of Allah's Name:

My Reflection Of Allah's Name:

"Call upon Allah or call upon the Most Merciful. Whichever (Name) you call - to Him belong the best names." - The Quran 17:110

Allah's Beautiful Names

⫸————————————————————→

DATE:

The Beautiful Name Of Allah:

Meaning Of Allah's Name:

Allah's Name In The Quran:

Explanation Of Allah's Name:

My Reflection Of Allah's Name:

"Call upon Allah or call upon the Most Merciful. Whichever (Name) you call - to Him belong the best names." - The Quran 17:110

Allah's Beautiful Names

>>>———————————————→

DATE:

The Beautiful Name Of Allah:

Meaning Of Allah's Name:

Allah's Name In The Quran:

Explanation Of Allah's Name:

My Reflection Of Allah's Name:

"Call upon Allah or call upon the Most Merciful. Whichever (Name) you call - to Him belong the best names." - The Quran 17:110

Allah's Beautiful Names

>>> ———————————————————→

DATE:

The Beautiful Name Of Allah:

Meaning Of Allah's Name:

Allah's Name In The Quran:

Explanation Of Allah's Name:

My Reflection Of Allah's Name:

"Call upon Allah or call upon the Most Merciful. Whichever (Name) you call - to Him belong the best names." - The Quran 17:110

Allah's Beautiful Names

>>>————————————————→

DATE:

The Beautiful Name Of Allah:

Meaning Of Allah's Name:

Allah's Name In The Quran:

Explanation Of Allah's Name:

My Reflection Of Allah's Name:

"Call upon Allah or call upon the Most Merciful. Whichever (Name) you call - to Him belong the best names." - The Quran 17:110

Allah's Beautiful Names

>>>———————————————————————>

DATE:

The Beautiful Name Of Allah:

Meaning Of Allah's Name:

Allah's Name In The Quran:

Explanation Of Allah's Name:

My Reflection Of Allah's Name:

"Call upon Allah or call upon the Most Merciful. Whichever (Name) you call - to Him belong the best names." - The Quran 17:110

Allah's Beautiful Names

>>>————————————————————————>

DATE:

The Beautiful Name Of Allah:

Meaning Of Allah's Name:

Allah's Name In The Quran:

Explanation Of Allah's Name:

My Reflection Of Allah's Name:

"Call upon Allah or call upon the Most Merciful. Whichever (Name)
you call - to Him belong the best names." - The Quran 17:110

Allah's Beautiful Names

>>>————————————————————→

DATE:

The Beautiful Name Of Allah:

Meaning Of Allah's Name:

Allah's Name In The Quran:

Explanation Of Allah's Name:

My Reflection Of Allah's Name:

"Call upon Allah or call upon the Most Merciful. Whichever (Name) you call - to Him belong the best names." - The Quran 17:110

Allah's Beautiful Names

>>>————————————————————>

DATE:

The Beautiful Name Of Allah:

Meaning Of Allah's Name:

Allah's Name In The Quran:

Explanation Of Allah's Name:

My Reflection Of Allah's Name:

"Call upon Allah or call upon the Most Merciful. Whichever (Name) you call - to Him belong the best names." - The Quran 17:110

Allah's Beautiful Names

>>>————————————————————————————→

DATE:

The Beautiful Name Of Allah:

Meaning Of Allah's Name:

Allah's Name In The Quran:

Explanation Of Allah's Name:

My Reflection Of Allah's Name:

"Call upon Allah or call upon the Most Merciful. Whichever (Name) you call - to Him belong the best names." - The Quran 17:110

Allah's Beautiful Names

>>> ⟶

DATE:

The Beautiful Name Of Allah:

Meaning Of Allah's Name:

Allah's Name In The Quran:

Explanation Of Allah's Name:

My Reflection Of Allah's Name:

"Call upon Allah or call upon the Most Merciful. Whichever (Name)
you call - to Him belong the best names." - The Quran 17:110

Allah's Beautiful Names

>>>————————————————————————→

DATE:

The Beautiful Name Of Allah:

Meaning Of Allah's Name:

Allah's Name In The Quran:

Explanation Of Allah's Name:

My Reflection Of Allah's Name:

"Call upon Allah or call upon the Most Merciful. Whichever (Name) you call - to Him belong the best names." - The Quran 17:110

Allah's Beautiful Names

>>>———————————————————→

DATE:

The Beautiful Name Of Allah:

Meaning Of Allah's Name:

Allah's Name In The Quran:

Explanation Of Allah's Name:

My Reflection Of Allah's Name:

"Call upon Allah or call upon the Most Merciful. Whichever (Name)
you call - to Him belong the best names." - The Quran 17:110

Allah's Beautiful Names

≫≫≫ ——————————————→

DATE:

The Beautiful Name Of Allah:

Meaning Of Allah's Name:

Allah's Name In The Quran:

Explanation Of Allah's Name:

My Reflection Of Allah's Name:

"Call upon Allah or call upon the Most Merciful. Whichever (Name) you call - to Him belong the best names." - The Quran 17:110

Allah's Beautiful Names

>>>———————————————————————————>

DATE:

The Beautiful Name Of Allah:

Meaning Of Allah's Name:

Allah's Name In The Quran:

Explanation Of Allah's Name:

My Reflection Of Allah's Name:

"Call upon Allah or call upon the Most Merciful. Whichever (Name) you call - to Him belong the best names." - The Quran 17:110

Allah's Beautiful Names

>>>————————————————————————→

DATE:

The Beautiful Name Of Allah:

Meaning Of Allah's Name:

Allah's Name In The Quran:

Explanation Of Allah's Name:

My Reflection Of Allah's Name:

"Call upon Allah or call upon the Most Merciful. Whichever (Name) you call - to Him belong the best names." - The Quran 17:110

Allah's Beautiful Names

>>>————————————————————→

DATE:

The Beautiful Name Of Allah:

Meaning Of Allah's Name:

Allah's Name In The Quran:

Explanation Of Allah's Name:

My Reflection Of Allah's Name:

"Call upon Allah or call upon the Most Merciful. Whichever (Name) you call - to Him belong the best names." - The Quran 17:110

Allah's Beautiful Names

→→→→————————————————————→

DATE:

The Beautiful Name Of Allah:

Meaning Of Allah's Name:

Allah's Name In The Quran:

Explanation Of Allah's Name:

My Reflection Of Allah's Name:

"Call upon Allah or call upon the Most Merciful. Whichever (Name) you call - to Him belong the best names." - The Quran 17:110

Allah's Beautiful Names

>>>——————————————————→

DATE:

The Beautiful Name Of Allah:

Meaning Of Allah's Name:

Allah's Name In The Quran:

Explanation Of Allah's Name:

My Reflection Of Allah's Name:

"Call upon Allah or call upon the Most Merciful. Whichever (Name) you call - to Him belong the best names." - The Quran 17:110

Allah's Beautiful Names

>>>————————————————→

DATE:

The Beautiful Name Of Allah:

Meaning Of Allah's Name:

Allah's Name In The Quran:

Explanation Of Allah's Name:

My Reflection Of Allah's Name:

"Call upon Allah or call upon the Most Merciful. Whichever (Name) you call - to Him belong the best names." - The Quran 17:110

Allah's Beautiful Names

DATE:

The Beautiful Name Of Allah:

Meaning Of Allah's Name:

Allah's Name In The Quran:

Explanation Of Allah's Name:

My Reflection Of Allah's Name:

"Call upon Allah or call upon the Most Merciful. Whichever (Name) you call - to Him belong the best names." - The Quran 17:110

Allah's Beautiful Names

>>>———————————————→

DATE:

The Beautiful Name Of Allah:

Meaning Of Allah's Name:

Allah's Name In The Quran:

Explanation Of Allah's Name:

My Reflection Of Allah's Name:

"Call upon Allah or call upon the Most Merciful. Whichever (Name) you call - to Him belong the best names." - The Quran 17:110

Allah's Beautiful Names

>>>————————————————————————→

DATE:

The Beautiful Name Of Allah:

Meaning Of Allah's Name:

Allah's Name In The Quran:

Explanation Of Allah's Name:

My Reflection Of Allah's Name:

"Call upon Allah or call upon the Most Merciful. Whichever (Name) you call - to Him belong the best names." - The Quran 17:110

Allah's Beautiful Names

>>>——————————————————————————>

DATE:

The Beautiful Name Of Allah:

Meaning Of Allah's Name:

Allah's Name In The Quran:

Explanation Of Allah's Name:

My Reflection Of Allah's Name:

"Call upon Allah or call upon the Most Merciful. Whichever (Name) you call - to Him belong the best names." - The Quran 17:110

Allah's Beautiful Names

>>>———————————————————>

DATE:

The Beautiful Name Of Allah:

Meaning Of Allah's Name:

Allah's Name In The Quran:

Explanation Of Allah's Name:

My Reflection Of Allah's Name:

"Call upon Allah or call upon the Most Merciful. Whichever (Name) you call - to Him belong the best names." - The Quran 17:110

Allah's Beautiful Names

>>>————————————————————>

DATE:

The Beautiful Name Of Allah:

Meaning Of Allah's Name:

Allah's Name In The Quran:

Explanation Of Allah's Name:

My Reflection Of Allah's Name:

"Call upon Allah or call upon the Most Merciful. Whichever (Name) you call - to Him belong the best names." - The Quran 17:110

Allah's Beautiful Names

>>>———————————————————→

DATE:

The Beautiful Name Of Allah:

Meaning Of Allah's Name:

Allah's Name In The Quran:

Explanation Of Allah's Name:

My Reflection Of Allah's Name:

"Call upon Allah or call upon the Most Merciful. Whichever (Name) you call - to Him belong the best names." - The Quran 17:110

Allah's Beautiful Names

>>>———————————————————→

DATE:

The Beautiful Name Of Allah:

Meaning Of Allah's Name:

Allah's Name In The Quran:

Explanation Of Allah's Name:

My Reflection Of Allah's Name:

"Call upon Allah or call upon the Most Merciful. Whichever (Name) you call - to Him belong the best names." - The Quran 17:110

Allah's Beautiful Names

>>>———————————————→

DATE:

The Beautiful Name Of Allah:

Meaning Of Allah's Name:

Allah's Name In The Quran:

Explanation Of Allah's Name:

My Reflection Of Allah's Name:

"Call upon Allah or call upon the Most Merciful. Whichever (Name) you call - to Him belong the best names." - The Quran 17:110

Allah's Beautiful Names

>>> ———————————————→

DATE:

The Beautiful Name Of Allah:

Meaning Of Allah's Name:

Allah's Name In The Quran:

Explanation Of Allah's Name:

My Reflection Of Allah's Name:

"Call upon Allah or call upon the Most Merciful. Whichever (Name) you call - to Him belong the best names." - The Quran 17:110

Allah's Beautiful Names

>>>———————————————————→

DATE:

The Beautiful Name Of Allah:

Meaning Of Allah's Name:

Allah's Name In The Quran:

Explanation Of Allah's Name:

My Reflection Of Allah's Name:

"Call upon Allah or call upon the Most Merciful. Whichever (Name) you call - to Him belong the best names." - The Quran 17:110

Allah's Beautiful Names

>>>⟶

DATE:

The Beautiful Name Of Allah:

Meaning Of Allah's Name:

Allah's Name In The Quran:

Explanation Of Allah's Name:

My Reflection Of Allah's Name:

"Call upon Allah or call upon the Most Merciful. Whichever (Name) you call - to Him belong the best names." - The Quran 17:110

Allah's Beautiful Names

>>>———————————————————→

DATE:

The Beautiful Name Of Allah:

Meaning Of Allah's Name:

Allah's Name In The Quran:

Explanation Of Allah's Name:

My Reflection Of Allah's Name:

"Call upon Allah or call upon the Most Merciful. Whichever (Name) you call - to Him belong the best names." - The Quran 17:110

Allah's Beautiful Names

>>>———————————————————→

DATE:

The Beautiful Name Of Allah:

Meaning Of Allah's Name:

Allah's Name In The Quran:

Explanation Of Allah's Name:

My Reflection Of Allah's Name:

"Call upon Allah or call upon the Most Merciful. Whichever (Name) you call - to Him belong the best names." - The Quran 17:110

Allah's Beautiful Names

DATE:

The Beautiful Name Of Allah:

Meaning Of Allah's Name:

Allah's Name In The Quran:

Explanation Of Allah's Name:

My Reflection Of Allah's Name:

"Call upon Allah or call upon the Most Merciful. Whichever (Name) you call - to Him belong the best names." - The Quran 17:110

Allah's Beautiful Names

>>>————————————————————→

DATE:

The Beautiful Name Of Allah:

Meaning Of Allah's Name:

Allah's Name In The Quran:

Explanation Of Allah's Name:

My Reflection Of Allah's Name:

"Call upon Allah or call upon the Most Merciful. Whichever (Name) you call - to Him belong the best names." - The Quran 17:110

Allah's Beautiful Names

DATE:

The Beautiful Name Of Allah:

Meaning Of Allah's Name:

Allah's Name In The Quran:

Explanation Of Allah's Name:

My Reflection Of Allah's Name:

"Call upon Allah or call upon the Most Merciful. Whichever (Name) you call - to Him belong the best names." - The Quran 17:110

Allah's Beautiful Names

>>>——————————————————→

DATE:

The Beautiful Name Of Allah:

Meaning Of Allah's Name:

Allah's Name In The Quran:

Explanation Of Allah's Name:

My Reflection Of Allah's Name:

"Call upon Allah or call upon the Most Merciful. Whichever (Name) you call - to Him belong the best names." - The Quran 17:110

Allah's Beautiful Names

>>>———————————————————————>

DATE:

The Beautiful Name Of Allah:

Meaning Of Allah's Name:

Allah's Name In The Quran:

Explanation Of Allah's Name:

My Reflection Of Allah's Name:

"Call upon Allah or call upon the Most Merciful. Whichever (Name) you call - to Him belong the best names." - The Quran 17:110

Allah's Beautiful Names

>>>————————————————→

DATE:

The Beautiful Name Of Allah:

Meaning Of Allah's Name:

Allah's Name In The Quran:

Explanation Of Allah's Name:

My Reflection Of Allah's Name:

"Call upon Allah or call upon the Most Merciful. Whichever (Name)
you call - to Him belong the best names." - The Quran 17:110

Allah's Beautiful Names

>>>————————————————→

DATE:

The Beautiful Name Of Allah:

Meaning Of Allah's Name:

Allah's Name In The Quran:

Explanation Of Allah's Name:

My Reflection Of Allah's Name:

"Call upon Allah or call upon the Most Merciful. Whichever (Name) you call - to Him belong the best names." - The Quran 17:110

Allah's Beautiful Names

>>>————————————————————>

DATE:

The Beautiful Name Of Allah:

Meaning Of Allah's Name:

Allah's Name In The Quran:

My Reflection Of Allah's Name:

"Call upon Allah or call upon the Most Merciful. Whichever (Name)
you call - to Him belong the best names." - The Quran 17:110

Allah's Beautiful Names

>>>———————————————————→

DATE:

The Beautiful Name Of Allah:

Meaning Of Allah's Name:

Allah's Name In The Quran:

Explanation Of Allah's Name:

My Reflection Of Allah's Name:

"Call upon Allah or call upon the Most Merciful. Whichever (Name) you call - to Him belong the best names." - The Quran 17:110

Allah's Beautiful Names

$\ggg$————————————————→

DATE:

The Beautiful Name Of Allah:

Meaning Of Allah's Name:

Allah's Name In The Quran:

Explanation Of Allah's Name:

My Reflection Of Allah's Name:

"Call upon Allah or call upon the Most Merciful. Whichever (Name) you call - to Him belong the best names." - The Quran 17:110

Allah's Beautiful Names

>>>————————————————————>

DATE:

The Beautiful Name Of Allah:

Meaning Of Allah's Name:

Allah's Name In The Quran:

Explanation Of Allah's Name:

My Reflection Of Allah's Name:

"Call upon Allah or call upon the Most Merciful. Whichever (Name) you call - to Him belong the best names." - The Quran 17:110

Allah's Beautiful Names

DATE:

The Beautiful Name Of Allah:

Meaning Of Allah's Name:

Allah's Name In The Quran:

Explanation Of Allah's Name:

My Reflection Of Allah's Name:

"Call upon Allah or call upon the Most Merciful. Whichever (Name) you call - to Him belong the best names." - The Quran 17:110

Allah's Beautiful Names

>>>———————————————————→

DATE:

The Beautiful Name Of Allah:

Meaning Of Allah's Name:

Allah's Name In The Quran:

Explanation Of Allah's Name:

My Reflection Of Allah's Name:

"Call upon Allah or call upon the Most Merciful. Whichever (Name) you call - to Him belong the best names." - The Quran 17:110

Allah's Beautiful Names

>>>————————————————————→

DATE:

The Beautiful Name Of Allah:

Meaning Of Allah's Name:

Allah's Name In The Quran:

Explanation Of Allah's Name:

My Reflection Of Allah's Name:

"Call upon Allah or call upon the Most Merciful. Whichever (Name) you call - to Him belong the best names." - The Quran 17:110

Allah's Beautiful Names

⟫⟫⟫————————————→

DATE:

The Beautiful Name Of Allah:

Meaning Of Allah's Name:

Allah's Name In The Quran:

Explanation Of Allah's Name:

My Reflection Of Allah's Name:

"Call upon Allah or call upon the Most Merciful. Whichever (Name) you call - to Him belong the best names." - The Quran 17:110

Allah's Beautiful Names

>>>———————————————————>

DATE:

The Beautiful Name Of Allah:

Meaning Of Allah's Name:

Allah's Name In The Quran:

Explanation Of Allah's Name:

My Reflection Of Allah's Name:

"Call upon Allah or call upon the Most Merciful. Whichever (Name) you call - to Him belong the best names." - The Quran 17:110

Allah's Beautiful Names

>>>———————————————————>

DATE:

The Beautiful Name Of Allah:

Meaning Of Allah's Name:

Allah's Name In The Quran:

Explanation Of Allah's Name:

My Reflection Of Allah's Name:

"Call upon Allah or call upon the Most Merciful. Whichever (Name) you call - to Him belong the best names." - The Quran 17:110

Allah's Beautiful Names

>>>————————————————————→

DATE:

The Beautiful Name Of Allah:

Meaning Of Allah's Name:

Allah's Name In The Quran:

Explanation Of Allah's Name:

My Reflection Of Allah's Name:

"Call upon Allah or call upon the Most Merciful. Whichever (Name) you call - to Him belong the best names." - The Quran 17:110

Allah's Beautiful Names

→→→————————————————→

DATE:

The Beautiful Name Of Allah:

Meaning Of Allah's Name:

Allah's Name In The Quran:

Explanation Of Allah's Name:

My Reflection Of Allah's Name:

"Call upon Allah or call upon the Most Merciful. Whichever (Name) you call - to Him belong the best names." - The Quran 17:110

Allah's Beautiful Names

>>>———————————————————————————→

DATE:

The Beautiful Name Of Allah:

Meaning Of Allah's Name:

Allah's Name In The Quran:

Explanation Of Allah's Name:

My Reflection Of Allah's Name:

"Call upon Allah or call upon the Most Merciful. Whichever (Name) you call - to Him belong the best names." - The Quran 17:110

Allah's Beautiful Names

>>> ———————————————→

DATE:

The Beautiful Name Of Allah:

Meaning Of Allah's Name:

Allah's Name In The Quran:

Explanation Of Allah's Name:

My Reflection Of Allah's Name:

"Call upon Allah or call upon the Most Merciful. Whichever (Name) you call - to Him belong the best names." - The Quran 17:110

Allah's Beautiful Names

>>>————————————————————————→

DATE:

The Beautiful Name Of Allah:

Meaning Of Allah's Name:

Allah's Name In The Quran:

Explanation Of Allah's Name:

My Reflection Of Allah's Name:

"Call upon Allah or call upon the Most Merciful. Whichever (Name) you call - to Him belong the best names." - The Quran 17:110

Allah's Beautiful Names

>>>————————————————————→

DATE:

The Beautiful Name Of Allah:

Meaning Of Allah's Name:

Allah's Name In The Quran:

Explanation Of Allah's Name:

My Reflection Of Allah's Name:

"Call upon Allah or call upon the Most Merciful. Whichever (Name) you call - to Him belong the best names." - The Quran 17:110

Allah's Beautiful Names

>>>———————————————————————→

DATE:

The Beautiful Name Of Allah:

Meaning Of Allah's Name:

Allah's Name In The Quran:

Explanation Of Allah's Name:

My Reflection Of Allah's Name:

"Call upon Allah or call upon the Most Merciful. Whichever (Name) you call - to Him belong the best names." - The Quran 17:110

Allah's Beautiful Names

⫸⫸⫸———————————————→

DATE:

The Beautiful Name Of Allah:

Meaning Of Allah's Name:

Allah's Name In The Quran:

Explanation Of Allah's Name:

My Reflection Of Allah's Name:

"Call upon Allah or call upon the Most Merciful. Whichever (Name)
you call - to Him belong the best names." - The Quran 17:110

Allah's Beautiful Names

>>>————————————————————————→

DATE:

The Beautiful Name Of Allah:

Meaning Of Allah's Name:

Allah's Name In The Quran:

Explanation Of Allah's Name:

My Reflection Of Allah's Name:

"Call upon Allah or call upon the Most Merciful. Whichever (Name)
you call - to Him belong the best names." - The Quran 17:110

Allah's Beautiful Names

$\ggg\!\!\!\longrightarrow$

DATE:

The Beautiful Name Of Allah:

Meaning Of Allah's Name:

Allah's Name In The Quran:

Explanation Of Allah's Name:

My Reflection Of Allah's Name:

"Call upon Allah or call upon the Most Merciful. Whichever (Name) you call - to Him belong the best names." - The Quran 17:110

Allah's Beautiful Names

>>>————————————————→

DATE:

The Beautiful Name Of Allah:

Meaning Of Allah's Name:

Allah's Name In The Quran:

Explanation Of Allah's Name:

My Reflection Of Allah's Name:

"Call upon Allah or call upon the Most Merciful. Whichever (Name) you call - to Him belong the best names." - The Quran 17:110

Allah's Beautiful Names

>>> ⟶

DATE:

The Beautiful Name Of Allah:

Meaning Of Allah's Name:

Allah's Name In The Quran:

Explanation Of Allah's Name:

My Reflection Of Allah's Name:

"Call upon Allah or call upon the Most Merciful. Whichever (Name) you call - to Him belong the best names." - The Quran 17:110

Allah's Beautiful Names

>>>——————————————————→

DATE:

The Beautiful Name Of Allah:

Meaning Of Allah's Name:

Allah's Name In The Quran:

Explanation Of Allah's Name:

My Reflection Of Allah's Name:

"Call upon Allah or call upon the Most Merciful. Whichever (Name) you call - to Him belong the best names." - The Quran 17:110

Notes

Notes

Thank you so much for purchasing the
Asma ul Husna Journal.

If you liked this journal, please leave a
review on Amazon or share your comments on
www.muslimjournals.com

Jazakallah khair for spreading the joy!

Asma ul Husna Journal
By Muslim Journals

Learn more about the author and get some freebies on our
website at www.muslimjournals.com. We offer many
more journals for men, women, teens, and kids.

Some of the options you will find include:

- Quran Journals
- Hadith Journals
- Dua Journals
- Salah Journals
- Sawm Journals
- Asma ul Husna Journals

- Shukr Journals
- Barakah Journals
- Niyyah Journals
- Halaqa Journals
- Ramadan Journals
  And many more!

Made in the USA
Middletown, DE
21 February 2022